IN OLD PHOTOG
BRITA

BLETCHLEY

PAST & PRESENT

ROBERT COOK

SUTTON PUBLISHING

Sutton Publishing Limited
Phoenix Mill · Thrupp · Stroud
Gloucestershire · GL5 2BU

First published 2004

Copyright © Robert Cook, 2004

Title page photograph:
Aerial view of Bletchley town centre,
c. 1930 (*Simmons Aerofilms*)

British Library Cataloguing in Publication Data
A catalogue record for this book is available from the
British Library.

ISBN 0-7509-3445-X

Typeset in 10.5/13.5 Photina.
Typesetting and origination by
Sutton Publishing Limited.
Printed and bound in England by
J.H. Haynes & Co. Ltd, Sparkford.

Water Eaton Lane, *c.* 1910. (*Pam Essam*)

CONTENTS

Bletchley Park display of an old postbox and the German submarine replica from the film *Enigma*. The captured submarine *U-559* provided the code book vital to Bletchley Park's wartime code-breaking efforts. (*Robert Cook*)

INTRODUCTION

Of Bletchley, Arthur Mee observed in his classic 1920s study of Buckinghamshire, 'The railway has not destroyed its rural charm', adding 'Could the Romans resume their march along the Roman Watling Street a mile away they would find much here in the natural scene that they would recognise.' But since that was written much has changed. Another charming study by Clement Shorter in 1910 observed: 'From Newton Longville we go to Bletchley and Fenny Stratford . . . both being associated with Browne Willis, the antiquary. His wife is buried in the church at Bletchley and he is buried at Fenny Stratford. Now there is a closer alliance, for since the development of the railway works at Bletchley it has ceased to be a village and has practically grown into Fenny Stratford . . . Bletchley Park and the manor came into the hands of Browne Willis's grandfather, Dr Thomas Willis, in 1674. Browne Willis was Lord of the Manor from 1724 until his death. He repaired and decorated Bletchley church and did much for Fenny Stratford, reviving its market and rebuilding its church after the latter had been destroyed by fire in 1746.'

George Temple Melville, Marquess of Buckingham, supported the Grand Junction Canal project that reached Fenny Stratford in 1800, which benefited trade and growth. Meanwhile Bletchley village, a mile south-west, awaited its moment, which came when railways usurped a variety of stagecoach services. Though it would do little good for their canal, the Temple family obstructed Robert Stephenson's idea of taking the London–Birmingham railway through Buckingham, therefore a route through Bletchley offered the easiest option. The line opened in 1838, with Thomas Brassey's Oxford branch connecting with Bletchley in 1851. Fenny Stratford's fate was sealed.

Inevitably the railway was going to take its toll on rural charm. Tennyson observed the symbolic truth that railways represented 'the ringing grooves of change'. The Bletchley referred to in Ron Staniford's new *Bletchley Gazette*, on Saturday 25 November 1933, was a very different place to Shorter's or Mee's. Hitler had recently come to power, so more great changes were afoot. For the time being, however, there was optimism. Staniford's leader boasted: 'Your Own Local Newspaper At Last, "*The Gazette*" At Your Service'. The report continued with a parochialism that would not endure under his enlightened leadership: 'A newspaper published in Bletchley, for Bletchley people.' A hint of the founder's and editor's cosmopolitan outlook was there in the detail: 'Do not confuse us when we talk of Bletchley. We mean it in its wider sense, and seek to include in it the surrounding smaller villages from Woburn Sands to Winslow.'

Ron Staniford was going to have his idealism tested to extremes when war clouds gathered. The same inaugural issue of the *Gazette* carried a report 'Christians at War', including a letter from the Revd J.R.C. Forrest. He wrote: 'In spite of all your foolish resolutions at Oxford University or Labour Conferences, they will not be worth a snap of the fingers when Germany gets on her legs. Germany held up 30

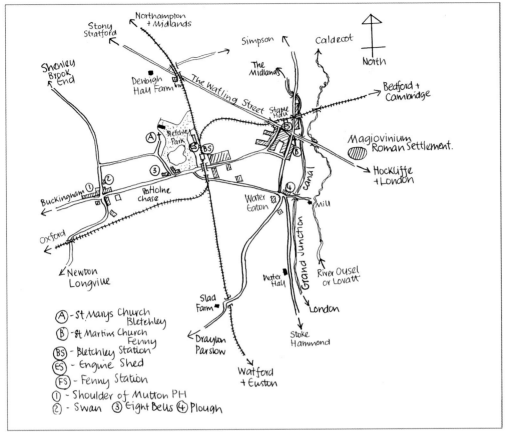

Bletchley and Fenny Stratford sketch map, late 1880s. The township of Fenny clustered around the Watling Street, the crossroad (Newport Pagnell to Leighton Buzzard), the canal and the river. Bletchley is beginning to develop to the east of the station – expansion to the west is prevented by Bletchley Park. The hamlet of Far Bletchley had cottages clustered around the Plough public house. Water Eaton is a hamlet on its own. (*Andrew Shouler*)

nations in the last war. It took nearly the whole civilised world to beat them, and they are not beaten yet . . . England has never been able to keep out of wars. . . . I think we should take the advice of that great English soldier . . . Oliver Cromwell, when he said: "Trust in God and keep your powder dry".' Ron Staniford took a different view, once telling me that there was good in everyone. When asked at a meeting what he would do if the Nazis shot his parents, he said 'Nothing'. He spent the Second World War as a conscientious objector and running his newspaper. This publication, by a self-taught journalist and extraordinary entrepreneur, is a fascinating, quaintly written record of the good old days and as illustrated in this 1930s account *Challenges to the Motorist*: 'A blanket of fog descended upon the district on Monday afternoon and lasted during the evening. Road traffic, especially on the Watling street . . . was rather disorganised, but there was surprisingly little delay in the rail services.' Other amusing items over the years included items falling off overloaded lorries and a man taking his trousers down before cuddling a policeman. However, as the war advanced there were sadder tales. These were relieved a little by the likes of Deanna Durbin and Pat O'Brien on screen at the County Cinema, Fenny Stratford, in *His Butler's Sister*.

Among lesser difficulties in wartime Bletchley was a report of 'Rat Menace' in June 1944, with these vermin accounting for 2 million tons of food destroyed or fouled nationally. The *Gazette* asked every man, woman and child to be a rat reporter. With Hitler on the run, Bletchley was as optimistic as the rest of Britain, joining in plans for a glorious future, but there were going to be struggles well into the 1950s.

Well-situated in the Ouzel Valley, Bletchley had expanded easily toward Fenny, with Bletchley Urban District Council taking responsibility for Fenny on 16 May 1911. Still predominantly a farming area in 1939, the main industries for the last hundred years had been bricks and railways. However, a hive of activity, focusing on Bletchley Park and Rickley Lane RAF camp, meant there was no going back. By 1966 there were fifteen firms from London, including S.S. White, Scott sausage and cooked meats, Terrapin and Rodex. The town took an incredible 42 per cent of its rateable value from industry and commerce and was a target for London overspill. Yet there were concerns that if it did not start building houses for people already resident, there would be problems. The local paper cited a woman who'd had three babies since applying for a home and was still waiting. Not surprisingly there was resentment towards newcomers, who saw life very differently, coming as they did to a country town with modern homes that were in stark contrast to the crowded slums of a postwar London (which had been painfully slow in meeting the needs of the homeless, though not so slow opening the way for property developments like Centre Point). London was becoming less of a place for Londoners and Bletchley less of a home for what some newcomers referred to as 'Carrot Crunchers'. The world was changing. Milton Keynes, the country's biggest ever overspill project, was on its way. Dr A.A. Clay of Newport Pagnell Urban Council said that Bletchley Road was one good reason for having an atom bomb if only the people could be moved out first!

On 20 January 2002 *Milton Keynes on Sunday* (now *MK News*) reported on a scheme based on the re-opening of the Oxford–Cambridge railway line. This was to involve demolition of Sherwood Drive's police and fire stations and major expansion of the railway station. The newspaper said that if the plan went ahead, these facilities would be located outside Bletchley and the whole railway station would be turned around. Railtrack's Midland Media manager said they had no concrete plans, 'but that does not mean it is not going to happen'. Now Railtrack is no more. How the mighty sometimes fall; nothing is certain, not even the past and this book presents just another view. Views, personal and practical, are always changing. Forty-three years ago Fred Constable came to a very different Bletchley: 'I went to work at Dyson Die Castings. There was a farmyard near our house, and the old Shoulder of Mutton. The road has been modernised. Things have got out of hand a bit, but I wouldn't go anywhere else.'

Robert Cook
November 2003

1

Whaddon Way

Whaddon Chase hunting folk in Newton Road, December 1970. (*Reg Knapp*)

The Normans brought a new order in 1066, Whaddon Manor passing to, among others, the Giffard family. Margaret Giffard married Robert Piggott and he took over the manor in the sixteenth century. Before the enclosures there was a great expanse of woodland and a chase, open land favourable for pursuing game from horseback. Thus began the tradition of the Whaddon Chase so enthusiastically pursued by later incumbents of the manor, the Selby Lowndes.

William Selby Lowndes, Shire Knight, became chairman of Queen Anne's 'Ways and Means Committee' and it was said that he liked to diminish others. The family's obsession, combined with poor estate management, forced sale to the McCorquodale's in 1897. The chase had covered 192 square miles from Aylesbury to Wolverton, relying very much on deferential farmers. Bert and Syd Illing at Salden broke the mould in 1927 by firing on a hunting party which included the Prince of Wales. Farmer R.W. Monk spoke for the old order when he told the local NFU farmers' dinner that 'No other farmers would offend a Prince as the Illings had done'. However, war was on the way and another massive assault on old ways. These are ironically commemorated in the naming of a major 1950s estate spine road on the western side of town: Whaddon Way. Symbols of this bygone age can be seen all the way down to the railway station, which really marked the new beginning.

Whaddon Way Garage at the junction with Buckingham Road during renovations in May 1997. It was originally a busy workshop, Renault dealership and filling station, but new road systems diverted traffic and led to a steady decline. (*Robert Cook*)

The scene in May 2003 is much changed after the filling station was demolished for Buckingham Court flats in December 2002. Advertised as an exclusive development, it is clearly money that does the excluding as Bletchley has become a very expensive suburb of Milton Keynes offering rich pickings for developers. (*Robert Cook*)

Early days. This brand new image of Castles Estate Shopping Centre, off Whaddon Way, is a very typical design from the 'all mod cons' 1960s. (*Pamela Essam*)

The scene is little changed today. The wider-angle shot shows some improved paving, flower tubs and the community centre. (*Robert Cook*)

Gas lights are a sign of modern times in this view of Bletchley village on the Buckingham Road in the early 1900s. Donald Fraser Blane, who emigrated to Canada, recalls: 'Because electricity did not come until 1930 gas was used for most homes for lighting and cooking. The largest customer was the railway company. Mr Jasper Cook, the gas works manager, engineer and secretary, gave me a job as office boy.' Gas meters were set to deliver slightly less than the coin value, so when the collector and his youthful assistant took their 'copper truck' around once a month, they would give customers a much-looked-forward-to 'rebate' which could be used for a little luxury or toward future gas supply. (*Pamela Essam*)

The road layout appears little changed in today's scene, but the thatched cottages have gone. More modern dwellings hide behind the high hedge and double yellow lines indicate that the road can be quite busy. (*Robert Cook*)

Looking across the Newfoundout, toward the railway line, station and a glimpse of the Oxford branch line junction, *c*. 1910. Youngsters in the foreground indicate this was a popular recreation space as well as a watering hole for railway locomotives and a dumping ground for ashes, as Martin Blane discovered when he fell in one day and got covered in slime. (*Pam Essam*)

Almost the same outlook today, from the mothballed Oxford branch viaduct to avoid the dense undergrowth. The west coast main line can just be seen. Milton Keynes and Bucks County Council support the line reopening, but the Strategic Rail Authority lacks funds; the only hope is that planned city expansion will get the money from developers. Thus, the transport situation must get worse in proportion to whatever new rail services will be provided so that, overall, travel will remain just as challenging. Officially Britain's railways are the most expensive and worst in Europe, often with dirty crowded carriages, with more fare rises and cuts in the offing. It said much about Britain's ability to run a railway when the Labour government cut the Oxford–Cambridge line in 1967 just as Milton Keynes new town was being planned. Robert Maxwell MP called it an odd case for closure when the line was already in profit, and when only eight years earlier a massive viaduct had been completed to improve cross-country freight services through Bletchley. (*Robert Cook*)

View of the old Shoulder of Mutton, also known as The Three Trees, and the winding road out towards Buckingham, *c.* 1900. Gina Ward recalls that 'going into the Shoulder you stepped down. You had to keep your head down all the way to the bar. That was the only place you could stand up.' This was farming country, hence the name, and the pub was a favourite watering hole. The picture is taken from the Shenley Road side, with Newton Road leading off left. Eddie Hancock, aged twelve, used to deliver the papers here and along Buckingham Road for WH Smith. 'They supplied a bike and I got 12s 6d a week.' (*Pam Essam*)

The Shoulder of Mutton closed in 1962 and the building was demolished, ending two centuries of drinking. Today's scene shows that the house on the corner of Newton Road survives but the road junction has been widened to allow for much heavier through traffic and estate traffic feeding on to Buckingham Road. A new Shoulder of Mutton, with a large car park off Shenley Road, was built on the opposite side of the road, just behind where this picture was taken, and was subsequently renamed The Three Trees. (*Robert Cook*)

Looking in the opposite direction, almost from the same spot as the previous two pictures, along Buckingham Road into Bletchley Road, showing Major's Hill, *c.* 1910. The road is very narrow, cutting between Colonel Whiteley's estate on the right and Bletchley Park, which is a bit further down on the left. (*Pam Essam*)

Viewed from the same spot today the road line is similar and the old house on the left has been modernised for shop use. Inevitably there has been considerable widening of the road. Whiteley's land is now a housing estate and more housing has been added on the opposite side of the road. (*Robert Cook*)

Turning into Shenley Road, and looking north, with the Swan Hotel dominating the scene, early 1900s. (*Pam Essam*)

Superficially everything looks much the same today, but the road surface is much improved, wider and with pavement. Yellow lines encourage us not to loiter with our cars, and estate side roads and houses can be glimpsed behind bushes that in the other image hid only fields. The Swan's bulk identifies the location but the old cottages have become the Shenley Hotel. (*Robert Cook*)

A short distance beyond the Swan the traveller can turn right from Shenley Road and cut across to here, where Church Green Road made its junction with Rickley Lane. This photograph, taken in about 1912, shows people facing very self-consciously toward the cameraman and holding very still. (*Pam Essam*)

People have once again become very conscious of the camera, but for different reasons. While photographing images of today I was regularly asked why I was in the street taking pictures around people's houses. Progress has created many new suspicions and anxieties; large hedges hide away Church Green Road's fine old houses which, behind all the greenery, look much the same as nearly a century ago. (*Robert Cook*)

St Mary's church, *c.* 1910. This large battlemented church tower stands just off Church Green Road, heading back down hill into town. The building, with decorated arcade between chancel and thirteenth-century chapel, is a little hidden by poplars and yews. The great doorway was built by Normans and Saxon builders pointed the Norman arch, giving it a boldly carved head as keystone, keeping the beak moulding and heads of Norman patricians and Saxon peasants. It is amazing to think the beautiful tower arch has stood for over half a millennium. (*Pam Essam*)

Mr Kemsey carved his name to claim credit for building the fine tower of St Mary's, still standing proudly in May 2003 after so many centuries. This is a place of great local history, where among many points of interest a fifteenth-century alabaster figure of Baron Grey of Wilton was placed. There is much more to be said of this church, but it is best to go and look. (*Robert Cook*)

Wilton Avenue, off Church Green Road, leads into Bletchley Park (viewed here from across the corner of the lake), in early twentieth-century glory. St Mary's church looms above the trees and bushes on the left. The swans enjoy tranquil waters in front of the great house and its jumbled features. (*Pam Essam*)

Nowadays the house is a heritage museum, after earning fame as Britain's wartime centre for code-breaking activities, and more recently through the theft of the Enigma machine. The lakeside view is much the same with swans and other bird life enjoying the lake's tranquillity. The house was built in 1860, and comprises half-timbered gables, oriels and a large domed Edwardian bay window. Financier Sir Herbert Leon bought it, commissioning extensions in 1883 and 1906. He was a friend of Lloyd George and a respected Liberal MP. Large estates like his were symbolic of the social order. (*Robert Cook*)

Back out on the Buckingham Road heading down towards the railway bridge, just before the junction with Church Green Road, early 1930s. The Brickhills mark the horizon, with gaslight and real horsepower denoting a slower age, but telegraph poles loom large and jaunty presaging a rush to faster and faster means of communication. (*Pam Essam*)

I had to wait a while for a break in the traffic to get a comparable shot today. The road is often busy, leading down to the railway and the centre. Sensibly householders have protected themselves from view and pollution by growing trees and hedges. The houses look much the same, however, except for the addition of TV aerials. Sleek electric lighting has replaced gas and telephone lines run underground. (*Robert Cook*)

The Eight Bells at the junction with Church Green Road, early twentieth century. This pub was popular with the Whaddon Chasers, with the great open space of Lord Leon's estate situated just beyond Hopcraft and Norris's building. One lady also recalled how, with teenage friends dressed in full skirts with stiff petticoats, bouffant or beehive hair and stilettos, 'the oldest looking one went in to buy cider and ten fags'. The roof of the Freeman Memorial Hall is prominent beyond the cottages. Though a Wesleyan Methodist church, it was named after James John Freeman, a meat and poultry trader from London. (*Martin Blane*)

On the same spot today there are a few changes. The Eight Bells has been feminised to become Eight Belles and given a modern makeover for a pub industry full of keen competition and novelty. It is no longer a place for old yokels or railwaymen to chew the fat. The merchant's building is now devoted to the grand industry of vehicle care, offering good value in tyres and carrying a poster warning that local police are on the lookout for defective ones. The grand bulk of the Cable & Wireless building stands above the greenery, centre right. (*Robert Cook*)

Looking west along Buckingham Road from the junction with Water Eaton Road, early 1900s. Bletchley Park's lodge gates look rather splendid on the right of the picture and an immaculate wall runs all the way along to the Freeman Memorial Hall and adjacent cottages. This part of the village had an abundance of tied cottages and labour was cheap enough to ensure all aspects of the Leon estate were well maintained. (*Pam Essam*)

Still recognisable as the same place today, but the lodge has gone and a ramshackle fence has replaced the old wall. The sturdy old cottages have also made way for modern structures. At least the Freeman Memorial Hall is still in fine fettle. (*Robert Cook*)

The pavilion, Bletchley Park, *c.* 1910. This was the scene of much upper-class revelry before two world wars began to erode the old order. Lord Leon was a generous overlord, allowing the pavilion and lawns to be used for local fetes and shows as well as opening up his grounds. Used also by the wartime Home Guard, the pavilion finished its days as the North Bucks Music Centre, having been in the grounds of what became the grammar school and, later on, the College of Further Education when the new city disposed of grammar schools. (*Pam Essam*)

The pavilion today is a sorry sight, run down and boarded up by builders working on a new college. These works make replication of the original shot impossible. (*Robert Cook*)

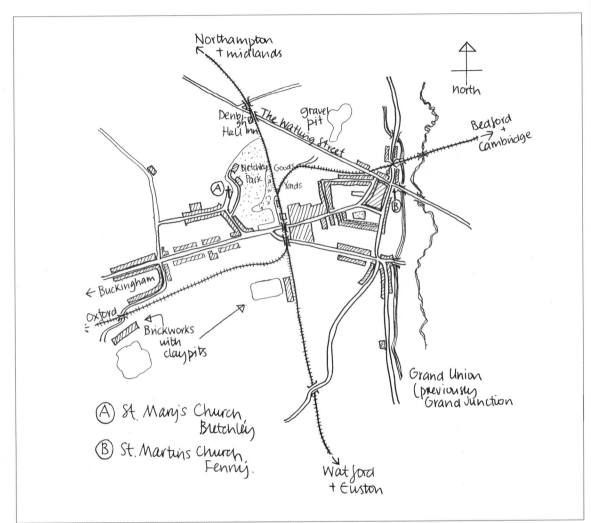

Sketch map of Bletchley and Fenny Stratford, 1920s. The towns just meet up. Ribbon building (notorious in the 1920s and 1930s) along the established roads can be seen particularly on the Buckingham Road, but there are plenty of open fields still to the north-west of Bletchley Park. (*Andrew Shouler*)

2

Permanent Way

An aerial view of Bletchley station, looking toward the town, 1920s. The completed London–Birmingham railway opened in 1838, sealing the fate of Fenny which had come to depend on stagecoach and canal. Stagecoaches had their last fling hereabouts ferrying rail passengers from Denbigh Hall to Rugby while the final metals were being laid. The coming of the Oxford and eventually Cambridge link made Bletchley an important junction and goods traffic flourished through the cross-country link. As Bletchley driver Fred Bateman observed, 'There was a big advantage in that the Oxford to Cambridge branch crossed so many main lines. It never should have closed. It wasn't Dr Beeching's idea or intention. . . . Before privatisation, when I was an area controller, [the railway] gave the passengers priority. . . . Nationalisation had been good because you came to feel you were all one.' (*Bletchley Voices*) In May 2003 railway chiefs admitted that passengers would have to face another five years before services are up to scratch.' Interestingly while £10 takes you 42 miles in Britain, in France it is 71.02 miles and in Italy 184.5 miles. All is a far cry from when Milton Keynes new town development was announced and H.C. Johnson, chairman of London Midland Railway, said that Bletchley was well served, they were building a new car park and that trains were vital in attracting new people to the area. (*Simmons Aerofilms*)

Bletchley loco shed, looking south, west of the main line, 6 April 1963. The original wood and iron structure was destroyed in a gale in 1876. It was rebuilt for six roads, with pits, and the station was also redeveloped in 1881, including construction of an overbridge replacing the subway. The presence of the diesel here warns that steam days are numbered. Driver Eddie Hancock, who fired a loco on the last day of steam working the Oxbridge line, recalled that 'In steam days there was so much pressure for speed, you worked from Bletchley to Euston, up to Camden, turned the engine round, with an hour to oil it before return. The fireman was busy smashing up his coal. Most jobs you had a comfortable

two hours unless you had a bunker engine. It could take 10–12 hours on a long goods train to London and back. There's not even a guard now. On the Electric Multiple Units you run into Euston and ten minutes later you are on your way out again.' (*Edwin Wilmshurst*)

Inset: There is no trace of the old engine sheds in this view from the same place today. This is H.C. Johnson's car park, so vital in '60s plans to make the railway the centre of modern Bletchley. When the British Transport Commission took over the LMS in 1948 it became responsible for Bletchley's sixty-seven engines and a coal bill for 950 tons a week. (*Robert Cook*)

A big BR tender engine on Bletchley turntable, 6 April 1963. Pam Essam remembers going down to the engine sheds to meet her dad coming in on his engine and having a ride on the turntable. The new water tank is just in view, holding 60,000 gallons. The original tank, by the station, was converted into overnight accommodation for drivers coming off shift and out of driving hours. (*Edwin Wilmshurst*)

Inset: There is little romance about this dingy corner of the car park that once was home to the water tower and turntable. The only evidence of glory days is a great concrete block which was once part of a buffer, cracked by a wayward loco falling from the turntable. (*Robert Cook*)

Station frontage, May 1962. This had been renovated ten years earlier. The completed viaduct is just visible, far right. When the line first opened there was a temporary terminus next to the Denbigh Hall pub. However, everything is temporary and this fine old station would soon be consigned to history. (*K. Barrow*)

Bletchley station today, functional but without grandeur, mystery or detail in design. When Bletchley town manager Mr J.F. Smithie prepared his development plan for Bletchley in 1967 the government was already talking of spending cuts which would affect plans for the area. So although Mr Smithie declared that 'Bletchley station is the key to the new town. There is no other place offering a service. Further north you can get only half the service.' British Railways was going further into decline and Barbara Castle cut the Oxbridge line. (*Robert Cook*)

Bletchley station in the early 1950s, from the end of the old no. 1 platform which carried services to Oxford, Banbury and Buckingham, the latter two destinations branching from Verney Junction. (*Initial Photographics*)

Platform 1 is no more, the alignment has been changed and the old station canopies have been demolished, along with the rambling brick buildings. Overhead cables crackle and a high-speed Virgin train thunders through. Richard Branson's company was indeed a virgin when it came to running railways, unlike so many old Bletchley hands who found their skills and experience redundant in the brave new world of privatisation. (*Robert Cook*)

A view through to the old booking hall, 27 April 1950. An array of sombre posters mentions regular trains, accidents and the carriage of dangerous goods. A local train, with wooden carriages, stands at the platform. In spite of nationalisation the rail company is advertised as London, Midland and Scottish Railways reminiscent of a time when privatisation worked a lot better. (*Initial Photographics*)

Inset: From the same spot today there is no chirpy ticket collector. Everyone just gets herded through the turnstiles; it cuts fare-dodging and saves on time and money. But is it human? (*Robert Cook*)

The late Ken Barrow, seen here working in the ticket office on 26 May 1955, was more than just a friendly hard-working man in the booking office, he was part of a service tradition and an excellent photographer, helping to record a way of Bletchley life so swiftly lost. (*Ken Barrow*)

Fortunately there are still friendly faces on Bletchley station. Darby Allan is one of the old school, and he is not alone. His mother was well known along the Buckingham branch where she ran Padbury station with great efficiency and friendliness. Darby went out of his way to help the author recreate some of the old railway scenes as they are today. (*Robert Cook*)

Bletchley station seen from a signal gantry and showing track skewed for the flyover then being built. The old carriage shed is visible far left, next to the Oxford branch, and cranes and burgeoning concrete structures indicate that the 1959 flyover project is under way. It is a wonderful example of Britain's complete incapacity for forward planning that this great work came so few years before the line was closed to all but a few rumbling stone trains and empty stock movements. British Railways, guided by penny-pinching governments, preferred to send cross country trains via London. No wonder rail freight was so uncompetitive. (*Author's Collection*)

A similar view from the viaduct in July 1991. Number one signal-box, where the likes of Sid Sellars worked the levers during the '50s has made way for the power box of an automated age. The large building, far right, was the old goods shed but is now a cement works. Overhead cables further indicate that these are modern times, along with a dearth of trains! (*Robert Cook*)

A clear view of major station redevelopment in 1959, with the new flyover in place, dwarfing the old signal-box and the bridge across Buckingham Road which will soon be gone. Bulldozer drivers look engrossed in their work re-sculpting the landscape while a smart Hillman Minx heads west along Buckingham Road. Platelayer Des Tunks recalls: 'Building the viaduct we worked all night. Archie Garner was ganger at Bletchley. The silly fools would go to the pub, the Park Hotel or the Working Men's Club, every evening break. They weren't safe doing that and coming back on that sort of work. Once you'd got the track out you had to go right through two shifts to get it ready. Bob North was the flag man keeping an eye out for the trains.' Doreen Dimmock remembers being kept awake by the constant 'bang, bang, bang' while they were setting the piles for the flyover. (*Colin Scott*)

Health and safety regulations prevent too close an approximation to the previous view today, but the railings near the Park Hotel show roughly the location of the new rail bridge over Buckingham Road. (*Robert Cook*)

3

Making Way

A Christian choir outside the Brunel Shopping Centre, June 1999. Much of the old town centre was bulldozed during the early 1970s to fit in with Milton Keynes which engulfed it. When development plans were announced in 1966, local MP Robert Maxwell said it was a big mistake to contemplate such a big city so near London. He would have preferred to see Bletchley continue with its own plans. Many locals, like Pauline Webb, take the view that the new town, home to 250,000 people over 25 years, has taken all the best away from Bletchley. Maxwell had argued for twin towns of Bletchley and Wolverton as the focus for development, with Bletchley having 100,000 people on 5,000 acres and Wolverton 75,000 on 3,600 acres instead of Crossman's 27,000 acres. There would be a monorail linking the two towns and the whole plan would help to rehouse 120,000 Londoners. But Crossman and his successor were in a hurry and wanted a prestige project, albeit under-funded as usual. An inquiry came to a quick decision, amid criticisms that it was a foregone conclusion – a view led by Maxwell.

Bletchley leaders were very disappointed that Bletchley did not become the centre of the new town. The government said the main purpose of the town, later known as Milton Keynes, was to provide housing and employment for people now living in London. Omerod said Bletchley had been doing that under the Town Development Act since 1951, the population rising from 10,000 to 23,000 in that time. It could easily expand in close proximity to the railway station and the A5. Some would argue that Bletchley has become that neglected suburb. But it has fought to keep its identity. (*Robert Cook*)

The Blane family outside their neat little railway cottage home in Railway Terrace, off Buckingham Road, early twentieth century. Bob Blane, eventual manager of Bletchley Co-op, is front right. (*Martin Blane*)

The same spot today presents one of radical change, with the high-tech Cable & Wireless building covering much of the old railway property site. Railway decline is common knowledge, but telecommunications have struggled to maintain an industry that they hoped would be ineluctable. (*Robert Cook*)

Moving down hill toward Bletchley Road, *c.* 1908. Just beyond the railway bridge are the gaunt lines of the Park Hotel rising above the quaint little street scene; a local carter trundling along completes the picture. Youngsters are having fun near the turning into the goods yard. (*Pam Essam*)

Only a glimpse of the Park Hotel, through the new bridge supports, identifies this as the same place today. The old railings have gone, replaced by a massive brick-retaining wall. The elegant lines of concrete flyover complete this almost tunnel view. Trees still shroud some of the older buildings, but the old shops are long gone, the Brunel Centre having cut Bletchley Road in half, with a large roundabout and dual carriageway replacing the goods shed drive, to the left. This new road made a connection with Watling Street and Fenny, with a branch looping around Brunel Centre, back on to Bletchley Road and Fenny beyond. The town-centre section of Bletchley Road was renamed Queensway in 1965. (*Robert Cook*)

Bletchley Road viewed from the railway bridge, *c.* 1958. Park Hotel and the exit from Duncombe Street make familiar landmarks. One of the newer vehicles in the London Brick Company fleet of the day, an AEC Mercury, approaches the camera. The line of old tin shops stretches out just beyond the railings. In those days names like Baldry for cycles and taxis, Cowlishaw for clothes, Emerton the jeweller, Bentina the dairy and Bollon's the tobacconist were household names, tried and trusted by the close-knit community. (*K. Barrow*)

The same place today shows just how much impact the 1959 flyover had on local scenery. It was part of a plan to promote freight services and development of Swanbourne sidings. Constructed just before the Beeching axe, it served little purpose because a cash-strapped and union-dominated Labour government chose the easy course of closing the Oxford–Cambridge line just at the moment Milton Keynes was designated. So much for Harold Wilson's 'white hot technological revolution'. The Brunel Centre and dual carriageway represent that, I suppose! (*Robert Cook*)

An uncluttered view of the new flyover, looking toward the town centre, *c.* 1958. There's still a lot of tidying up to do. The old main line London–Birmingham railway bridge is still *in situ*, as well as the station approach. A mighty crane points skyward, symbolic of the power and ingenuity required for such great earthworks. (*Author's Collection*)

The scene is much transformed today. The new station approach is to the left of the camera-man, the old approach being filled by the police station, an embankment and pedestrian steps. A more substantial bridge spans the dual carriageway and carries more lines. Alas British Railways, born on 1 January 1948, is no more. The engine crossing the bridge, in this recent picture, bears the logo Virgin. Bletchley has a good rail safety record, with only one serious accident on Friday 13 October 1939. Driver Haynes, on the 19.50 Euston–Stranraer express, through heavy rain and blackout missed a home signal, colliding with Irving Butler's shunting engine which had been busy assembling carriages to the Inverness train. Butler and three others were killed and forty injured. Station Inspector Walter Nursaw saw it coming. His warning call saved lives. (*Robert Cook*)

This picture shows the old bridge still in place and the new rail road under construction. The grand new flyover rises to the left of the image, carrying the ill-fated Oxbridge freight line. A tank engine hisses away with a weight of carriages, steam making milky patterns in the sky. (*Robert Cook*)
Inset: This picture is taken from a very overgrown and litter-strewn bank to the right of the new

road, the exact same position being impossible to repeat without standing on the main line. Overhead power lines indicate that steam has been usurped by cleaner energy – that is if you overlook power-station pollution! The viaduct is obscured by trees. A brick-retaining wall adds the finishing touch to this modern view. (*Robert Cook*)

A Coles 20-ton crane hoists a bucket over the bridge works and a handsome Rover 90 swishes past the Park Hotel *en route* for town in this late 1950s scene. The old bridge with its meagre 12 ft 6 in height allowance will soon be gone. A workman's ladder rests against the Park Hotel and a dirty black BR tender loco backs toward the bridge, the driver studying a labourer standing casually upon a pillar.

Inset: The road today is realigned, the pavement outside Park Hotel cutting into the former carriage-way. A modern train with 'go faster' stripes roars over the bridge behind the mothballed viaduct. This defunct concrete masterpiece may yet see new life if Deputy Prime Minister John Prescott's plan to expand Milton Keynes out to Winslow gets the go-ahead and makes road congestion even worse than it is. (*Robert Cook*)

Bletchley Road, *c. 1920*. Many of Bletchley's first shops were adapted houses. This picture was taken from the pavement adjacent to the Working Men's Club. The goods yard entrance is clearly signed. Horse-pulled railway delivery carts were a familiar sight until after the war. Ray Akins availed himself of this work when the brickworks slowed down during the Depression years. Horses were also used for shunting, and blacksmith Bill King was a busy man. (*Colin Scott*)

Inset: The same place today shows little if any resemblance to the old days. Bletchley Road has been cut off by the Brunel Centre and further development is in hand. Shrubbery and pavement-widening have replaced the gateway in front of the Working Men's Club. The little way into the station goods yard has been lost to bulldozers cutting out a big roundabout and the dual carriageway of Saxon Street, heading north to the A5 Watling Street and Milton Keynes. (*Robert Cook*)

A late 1930s view from the top of Bletchley Road shopping centre, before redevelopment. Albert Street entrance and the Co-op are just visible in the middle distance, left. W. Davis's lorry would have been quite a juggernaut in its day but would now appear little more than a pick-up. Bletchley Road was so-called because it was the road to Bletchley, but by this time it was in Bletchley. To some, Bletchley Road, Bletchley, sounded silly, but the name change to Queensway still was a long way off.

Road traffic was clearly a novelty as it was possible to have petrol pumps in the town centre, just visible almost opposite the Co-op. (*Colin Scott*)
Inset: This is the view today, from outside Boots in the Brunel Centre. To be strictly accurate we would have to look from inside the chemist's shop to see exactly how the scene has changed. (*Robert Cook*)

Bletchley Road and the junction with Albert Street, late 1940s. The Co-op shows how much it has moved with the times, sporting an art-deco frontage. The sun must be shining because Rushdon the chemist, on the corner of Albert Street, has his blind down. Martin Blane recalls going in there to collect medicines for his parents in the 1930s: 'When he asked you what you wanted, it always sounded like he was saying "as mister"' [yes mister]. (*Pam Essam*)

The site has now been pedestrianised at the Brunel Centre end. New building work has altered this part of the street, but the Co-op is still in the same place, albeit without that marvellous frontage. Blooming trees obscure the opposite side of the road but a plethora of cars are just visible all along the kerbside. Rushdon's is now a craft shop with office space to let above. (*Robert Cook*)

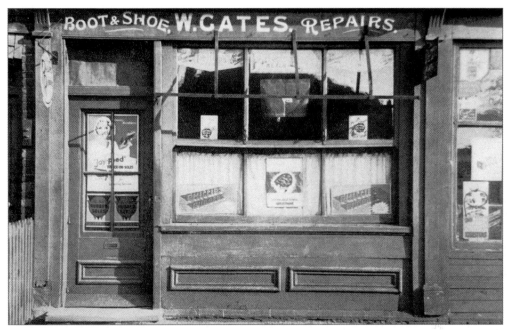

Bletchley & District Co-operative Society held its first meeting at Bletchley station on 10 December 1883, aiming to raise capital by selling 200 10-shilling shares. Mr Simmonds was elected president but had a fatal accident in the yard immediately afterwards and was replaced by Mr Piper at the second meeting on 31 December. The pioneers approached the owner of W. Gates's shop in Park Street, shown here, for a tenancy and business commenced in February 1884. (*Martin Blane*)

Park Street disappeared with the development of the Brunel Centre. Gates's shop site is now obliterated by these concrete walls along the pathway to Stephenson House and the bus station. (*Robert Cook*)

Co-op business flourished and the society soon moved on to these larger premises in neighbouring Albert Street, diversifying its activities. Unfortunately an arsonist destroyed this building and the Co-op moved to its present site in Queensway in 1927. (*Martin Blane*)

The old Albert Street site remains undeveloped, serving a useful purpose as a car park for the Co-op. The Sunlight Soap advert is kept in good order on the end wall where the Co-op once joined the terrace, reminding us of the sort of things that were once for sale hereabouts. (*Robert Cook*)

The paved area behind Brunel Centre, where Park Street used to cross, September 1995. The viaduct marks the horizon. Darkness, street lights and youngsters at bay help impart a hint of new city life. Thomas Cook's travel agent's sign glows invitingly, offering the prospect of getting away from it all. (*Robert Cook*)

These days the pace of change is rapid. This valuable little open space is being filled by a big new development, to include Wilkinson's cut-price store and a fitness centre. (*Robert Cook*)

Bletchley bus station, summer 1983, before Tory de-regulation ended the reliable reign of United Counties Omnibus Company which had depots in Bletchley and Stony Stratford. Here we see an immaculate line of Bristol VR buses on a busy day. However, if the bus did not come on time this can be a very windswept and cold place to wait and services were beginning to decline. (*Stephen Morris*)

Inset: Bletchley bus station on a quiet and grey Sunday afternoon, June 2003. Milton Keynes Development replaced County Architect Fred Pooley's vision for a modern city with public transport built in. Estates were constructed without a view to buses providing transport into them. MK Metro does a good job against the odds but services have received much criticism. Cars rule the streets. (*Robert Cook*)

Oliver Road playing fields, an area eventually home to the cattle market, seen here in about 1920 with a football match about to start. (*Bletchley Archaeological and Historical Society*)

Strictly speaking this picture should have been taken inside Sainsbury's. But using poetic licence the author preferred to stand on the other side of the building in front of the loading bay. This slightly different angle on to Oliver Road shows that there has been little change to the buildings' external appearance. (*Robert Cook*)

Bletchley Road, late 1940s. Pollards shop is far left and the old post office is just in view. Motor cars are beginning to make their presence felt. (*Pam Essam*)

From the same spot today great changes are noticeable. Modern buildings are more box-like. The street is quiet because it is Sunday, but the local retail parks and Central Milton Keynes Shopping Centre will be busy. Bletchley is no longer the main area and charity shops predominate in Queensway. (*Robert Cook*)

Oxford Street, *c. 1912*. A multiplicity of terraced homes sprang up as the railway town of Bletchley spread east. This one was named after one of its rail destinations. Young families blossomed and went out to play. The two tall girls in the front line of this pose are Doris (left) and Mabel Benton. (*Pam Essam*)

Oxford Street today, neat and tidy and with little external change, but not a child in sight. Its proximity to Queensway means there are double yellow lines and designated parking for residents. (*Robert Cook*)

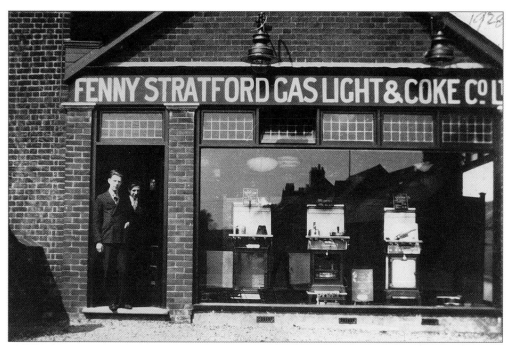

Fenny Stratford Gas Light and Coke Company offices, formerly Still's grammar school, are seen here on the corner of Cambridge Street and Queensway in 1928. Donald Fraser Blane and Jack Robinson are in the doorway. Donald recalls: 'The gas company would install a supply with a prepayment slot, three lights and a cooking stove free of charge.' This picture shows all the latest in gas cookers, such an improvement on the old ways. (*Donald Fraser Blane*)

Electricity and its offspring the computer are among the latest gadgets as empty premises on the same site today remind us. Nowadays life moves even faster and this shop will soon be something else. *Bletchley Gazette*'s call for a 'Bigger Brighter Bletchley' took quite a knock when it failed to become the centre of the new city. In 1966 Conservative parliamentary candidate Elaine Kellett said it was disgraceful so much countryside was being lost, and that Bletchley could only prosper if it was either at the centre of the new city or far enough away. (*Robert Cook*)

The Gardens, off Bletchley Road, showing Bletchley printing premises on the left, late 1940s. Princes Way was part of the 1970s improvements, cutting through the gardens and separating Cambridge Street from North Street. It is now a dual carriageway and a busy cut through from Bletchley Road to the A5 and Buckingham Road. Doreen Dimmock recalls: 'The gardens were lovely, with tennis courts on the left, putting green on the right, bowls and a sunken rose garden.' (*Pam Essam*)

Princes Way with what remains of the gardens far right. The pyramid of the leisure centre is popping its peak above the trees and bushes. (*Robert Cook*)

The snaking walkway to Bletchley Leisure Centre, summer 1990. The leisure centre was opened on 10 February 1973 by Dr Roger Bannister, provided under the leadership of Councillor Staniford, Chairman of the Health & Amenities Committee. The centre made TV news the following September when a young Chris Tarrant came with the ATV *Today* crew. A row had broken out over a plan to demolish the Queen's open-air pool which was bigger than the new leisure centre facility. Chairman of the 'Save the Pool' committee, David Lee, said Queen's pool should remain until an equal facility could be provided. The council refused to show ATV their new pool plans. Costs of demolishing Queen's pool were estimated at £30,000. (*Robert Cook*)

Now you see it, now you don't. The snake was demolished in the summer of 1999, revealing the pyramid in all its glory. Not quite Egypt, but rather exotic none-the-less. Pleasant pools complete the oasis effect here alongside the vibrant artery of Princes Way. (*Robert Cook*)

The massive concrete face of Princes Way multi-storey car park during its final days in summer 1995. Built mainly for leisure centre users, it was not the safest place to park the car, but very handy

for the market which moved down from Duncombe Street area in the 1970s. (*Robert Cook*)
Inset: Princes Way after the demolition of the multi-storey car park. (*Robert Cook*)

The great Princes Way car park, viewed from off Cambridge Street, a temple to the beloved motor car, is falling in May 1999. One man claimed damages when dust from the demolition work ruined his car's paintwork. A local newspaper was also criticised for comparing the imagery of destruction to

what was going on in Bosnia at the time. (*Robert Cook*)

Inset: September 1999 and the view is opened up, evoking memories of the once expansive central gardens. (*Robert Cook*)

Another wondrous image from Bletchley's sexy '70s! This market canopy is a good companion for the pyramid just around the corner. Though looking like a mini wonder of the world, I recall it did not keep out the cold winds when I was a market trader here. It was very much part of the desperate efforts to make Bletchley as glamorous as the money-no-object new city shopping centre. Rodwell, London & Provincial Properties were given responsibility for redevelopment and there were fears that the shops would outgrow demand. Woolworths in the centre of the block on the left was one of the first to leave. (*Colin Stacey*)

Vandals, or perhaps one might say lovers of good taste, destroyed the canopy in the mid-1990s and the market is now spread along Queensway. Nowadays Milton Keynes attracts the most earnest Saturday traders and Bletchley's market is more bread-and-butter, bargain clothes and greengrocers. Stalls now spread along Queensway and the Agora offers more cut-price opportunities. Meanwhile shops around this little square, which was built to make a second divide in the main road, are mainly charity second-hand outlets and estate agents. (*Robert Cook*)

4

Fenny Way

This image of Fenny Stratford from the 1930s shows the A5 Watling Street running almost diagonally from left to right, with Aylesbury Street cutting across, left to right, and joining Simpson Road at the crossroads. The Grand Union Canal marks another line; beyond that is the mighty gasworks and the furthest building, at the top of the picture, is nowadays the 'Pink Punters' club – a powerful symbol of how times have changed. The photo was taken from over Victoria Road, putting Church Street and George Street in clear view, along with a multitude of back garden secrets. (*Simmons Aerofilms*)

Bletchley Road from near the Studio Cinema, late 1940s. Doreen Dimmock remembers a man selling bread and buns here, and walking from Staple Hall Road to buy them. Bletchley Arms, left, was originally the site of a pub known as the Halfway House because of its location between the parishes of Bletchley and Fenny Stratford. Here we see cars beginning to make their presence felt. Everywhere looks neat and tidy. Just along on the right the little school is back to normal after struggling to accommodate wartime evacuees and being forced to work half-day shifts. (*Pam Essam*)

Externally the pub has gained a porch and balcony; otherwise the street scene looks very familiar, though there has been some infilling and the cars have changed. A medium size office block along to the left bears the new name of the road, Queensway House. (*Robert Cook*)

North Street, leading into Tavistock Street, *c.* 1960. The Oxford–Cambridge line runs along the embankment, and a little goods train looks like a tin plate Hornby toy, passing the signal-box on this once key route, linking main lines and the Oxford Clay Fletton brick fields. (*Ian Beckett*)

North Street, May 2003. The houses look much the same and this part of the old Oxford–Cambridge line is still open between Bletchley and Bedford, though you wait a long time to see a train and the signal-box has gone. A scrapyard around the corner in Tavistock means that this apparently quiet backwater can be busy with lorries. (*Robert Cook*)

Bletchley Road School with a pathway leading to Leon Recreation Ground and Fenny Cemetery. Eddie Hancock said: 'I wasn't highly educated. I went to the school in 1937. My education was disrupted by air raid sirens. We carried gas masks to school, across our shoulders. Every time the sirens went off we went to makeshift shelters. Eight bombs dropped near us at Bletchley Flettons. Mrs Fowler was wicked. She had a habit of lifting trousers and hitting thighs of 6–7 year olds. Mothers complained. Cookie, the headmaster, caned you on the rump and Miss Workman wouldn't let you write left handed. Cookie's nickname was Barrel because of his shape. He was reading "The horseman came riding up to the door . . .", making a wavy motion, getting carried away, I burst out laughing. He roared: "Come out here boy." I got caned. I learnt respect. That helped me in the army.' (*Colin Scott*)

Bletchley Road School is now Knowles First and Middle, Queensway Centre and Adult Learning. There were many promises of a better world after the Second World War and the 1944 Education Act provided for the building of large secondary modern schools to replace the old board schools. It would be many years before the new Leon School was built at Water Eaton. (*Robert Cook*)

Council offices, Victoria Road, at the junction with Vicarage Road and Queensway, late 1950s. At this point Bletchley was still centre of its own universe. Eddie Hancock opines: 'Bletchley has got very dilapidated, the buildings aren't looked after as they were. It used to be kept nice under Bletchley Council.' (*Robert Cook*)

It's Milton Keynes Council now and they have fine offices in the city centre. The old council building finds other purposes, here advertising bingo. The junction has been improved a little and the street lighting has changed, the postbox has gone, the new bollards lack charm, being designed to collapse if hit by the many more motorists, but otherwise the outlook is much the same. (*Robert Cook*)

Victoria Road, looking towards the junction with Queensway and Vicarage Road. Denmark Street junction, where Ackroyd Stewart invented the first diesel-type engine, before Diesel did, is visible left. A.C. Brinklow's newsagents was one of many good solid and thoroughly useful businesses in Fenny. Brian Sidebottom traded in Victoria Road for thirty years, retiring in April 2002. He said: 'You could buy anything in Victoria Road, there was the butcher's, the Co-op, and the electricity showrooms.

You could have your hair done. You could live off that street. But there were big changes. All traders suffered because of the multiples and Milton Keynes.' (*Colin Scott*)
Inset: This modern view shows the old shops have gone. Fryday's fish and chip chain has replaced Colgrove the butcher and the shops further down have been re-fronted in rectangular style. (*Robert Cook*)

The old Co-op store, almost demolished, 1999. Ackroyd Stewart's premises, a converted forge, was partly on this site and to the rear. A plaque commemorates his largely forgotten achievement. (*Robert Cook*)

The new Londis shop in Victoria Road has been built, incorporating some of the lower building, including the Ackroyd Stewart plaque on the wall just above the street sign for Denmark Street. (*Robert Cook*)

Fenny Stratford fire station, a converted church hall in Church Street, pictured in the late 1940s and featuring pre-war and wartime equipment. Massive reorganisation was afoot, including recruitment of new county firemen from London to work with the Buckinghamshire-retained crews. (*Colin Scott*)

Today's image shows the premises being used by the Bee's Knees Recruitment Agency. Milton Keynes is still a boom town, though heavily dependent on service industries. (*Robert Cook*)

Aylesbury Brewery Company was one of the biggest owners of tied public houses and this was a fine example in Aylesbury Street. To the left are the premises of Bletchley Motors, in an age when the British were still exporting Austin cars to Japan. Most cars on the street, like the Morris and Ford shown here, were British built. (*Bletchley Archaeological and Historical Society*)

The scene is much the same today, though the vehicles are foreign made. The car showrooms advertise a Japanese product and Aylesbury Brewery's name has vanished. In recent years it appeared that the brewery was worth more sold off in component form. The neat dormer windowpanes have been replaced by plain glass: such is the freedom of modern planning and the low value placed on conservation. The *News of the World* sign has gone, the last vestige of the now residential property's former trade. Behind this little abode was Pappy's Yard, named after Papworth who owned it. The Constable family lived here (see p. 96). (*Robert Cook*)

Aylesbury Street, early 1930s. We are all used to the sounds of traffic today but imagine how different those funny old cars, some chugging, others clattering, would sound to us if we were transported back in time to that street. What other sounds, long forgotten, would surprise us? They say it is multi-cultural now, but what of all the airs and graces then, posh-talking shop managers, gentlefolk and rustics, chirpy little urchins. It wasn't just the buildings that were different. What hopes and fears filled those people's minds? Inevitably, because travel was difficult and local job opportunities limited, the town would be more homogenous than it is today. (*Martin Blane*)

The same place today and there's much to be said about our hopes and fears, but the pace of life is so fast we scarcely have time to think. Modern cars swish by, status symbols to many now, or objects of envy and theft: as lethal as a gun but wielded casually by most. Glancing at the shops we see that old steady traders have made way for new city ways, including New City Heating. The premises are minus many chimneys – no need for the coalman and his cart or lorry now. The paintwork makes the buildings look bright and functional. (*Robert Cook*)

Looking south-west along Aylesbury Street, from Billy Golding's shop towards the junction with
Vicarage Road and Manor Road beyond, early 1930s. Mr Golding's motorbike and sidecar sports
an enigmatic sign: 'Stop me'. Why, what are you doing? Selling my famous ice cream, of course!
(*Colin Scott*). *Inset:* The same view today shows a little change. Inevitably the gas lamp has
gone. A car dealer occupies the old Golding site, a few of their wares on display next to the

filling station which dominates the landscape. Aylesbury Street is the place to buy bits and fuel for the beloved car. It is a common occurrence to see men drooling over and stroking the latest four-wheel drives on a Sunday afternoon hereabouts, with a number of dealers to choose from, and perhaps going on to enjoy a meal at one of the exotic local eating places. (*Robert Cook*)

The back of Billy Golding's motorbike combo reveals all he has to offer, again in the early 1930s. The Bull & Butcher pub signpost makes a landmark. It is said that Golding only made so much ice cream each year, devoting much time to work as a Special Constable. His little shop was full of certificates from his prize-winning entries into ice cream-making competitions. Because he won every year Walls offered him £46,000 for the recipe. He refused and the recipe died with him. He must have had a soul above money and no wish to retire from the work he loved. (*Colin Scott*)

Looking in the same direction today much has changed, but the pub sign remains to give us our bearings. (*Robert Cook*)

The Bletchley–Cambridge extension of the Oxford branch opened in 1862. This is Fenny Stratford station, less than a mile east of Bletchley station, in the early twentieth century. Fancy Gothic chimneys on the station buildings were designed to match the Duke of Bedford's estate. The sidings are still in place, taking over coal traffic from the nearby Grand Union Canal. (*Pam Essam*)

The scene looking east from Fenny bridge today is much changed, with the line single-tracked and sidings removed. A minimal passenger service continues to be operated by Silverlink as far as Bedford and there have been continuous campaigns to reopen the Oxford–Cambridge route in its entirety. This has encountered much opposition east of Bedford where residential encroachments seem to have made the idea unthinkable – it would be a lot easier to get a road built through people's property because the road lobby is more powerful. (*Robert Cook*)

Fenny Stratford level-crossing at Simpson Road, looking west as an LNWR Class 7 (an old D) hauls goods past the coal sidings and towards signalman Jack Bromfield's camera, late 1940s. (*Jack Bromfield*)

There is some similarity with the previous picture, but Fenny Stratford station is much reduced by the postwar attitude of cutting railways and overloading roads. (*Robert Cook*)

Looking east towards the crossroads and the Brickhills, this is Fenny Stratford High Street in about 1920, with distinctive London–Holyhead telegraph poles lining the route and bow window overhanging the street, marking the location of the old County or Palace Cinema. The three-storey building in the middle distance, left, was known as The Red House and was home to the local doctor. (*Pam Essam*)

The Red House is the major landmark seen from the same spot today. Doreen Dimmock said: 'Dr Carter lived here, he was a good maternity doctor. Our mothers paid into a panel scheme, Dr Carter was his own pharmacist.' The cluster of buildings, Brickhills on the horizon and the familiar straightness of the old Roman road also mark this out as the same place. Redevelopment has removed a house on the left and everything on the right, where a new estate and flats have replaced old terraces and a cinema. (*Robert Cook*)

St Martin's church, seen from Aylesbury Street, *c.* 1910. The building was down to the initiative of Lord of the Manor Browne Willis, who took a dim view of non-conformist chapels hereabouts. He encouraged donations, many from wealthy friends. His grandfather Thomas was a well-known doctor, born and dying on St Martin's Day and living in St Martin's Lane, London – hence the choice of name. (*Pam Essam*)

The original chapel was completed in 1730 and consecrated by the Bishop of Lincoln on 27 May 1730. A new aisle was built in 1823 and the church became the centre of a separate diocese from Bletchley in 1834. Seen here in June 2003, it looks better than ever in a corner of the great Milton Keynes conurbation that is surprisingly little changed. (*Robert Cook*)

Aylesbury Street, looking from the pavement by St Martin's church towards the junction with Simpson Road and the A5, *c.* 1930. The elderly lady in the shop doorway was *Bletchley Gazette* founder Ron Staniford's granny. She owned the shop with his aunt and the family name is painted on the wall running into Church Street.
(*Colin Scott*)

Inset: Over seventy years later the outlook is quite similar but the junction with the A5 has been opened up following demolition of Durran's shop on the corner of Aylesbury Street and the Rose and Crown pub in Simpson Road. Fenny Appliances has replaced the renowned Staniford name on the shop nearest the camera and the old horse trough has gone from the front of St Martin's. The Swan Hotel has also lost a few chimneys. (*Robert Cook*)

This picture takes us right up to the junction and turning right to look south along the A5 Watling Street, *c.* 1930. Mr Roberts, the AA man, was regularly stationed here and is almost in the centre. Gaslights are still in view but electricity is soon to arrive via the Northampton Electric Light Company – facilitating the introduction of traffic lights at this busy junction. Watson's Garage, next to the Bull Commercial Family Hotel, is visible on the right and the Brickhills are on the horizon. (*Colin Scott*)

Inset: There are local jokes about Milton Keynes resembling a fairground because it has so many roundabouts. Needless to say Fenny Stratford has its share, as we see here, after the traffic-light era. It's a double mini roundabout that dominates the scene today. Watson's Garage is still in view but now trading as Select Cars Sales. (*Robert Cook*)

This view looks the other way across the junction with Aylesbury Street and Simpson Road, early 1920s. From here we can see the other side of The Red House. The Rose and Crown pub stands separated from the Swan Hotel by the narrow Simpson Road, the Swan advertising its own garage. The small gathering in front of Durran's opticians includes two policemen from Fenny police station, which was along Simpson Road almost opposite the railway crossing. Doreen Dimmock remembers Mr Durran living with his old mother who 'used to dress like a Duchess, a great big silver fox fur around her shoulders'. (*Martin Blane*)

On a sunny January morning in 2003, shadow covers the double roundabout while sunlight reflects off the Swan. In the old days lorries often collided with this hotel, but the junction has had several improvements to cope with juggernauts. Mr Durran, his shop and his elderly mother are long gone, together with a way of life. By chance a policeman walks past the Swan, glancing like his predecessors at the camera, but his step shows that he has no time to lose. Policemen on the beat are a rare sight today and this one hasn't come from the local police station, which closed years ago. He is no doubt off to find his car and be away to some urgent call elsewhere. Authorities say beat officers aren't necessary because they rarely come within a mile of crime, but that ignores their deterrent effect. (*Robert Cook*)

The Bull Commercial Family Hotel, just south of the junction with Aylesbury Street and on a stretch of the A5 called the High Street. Watson's Garage looked after the guests' motor cars in an age when car ownership really was a mark of distinction. (*Martin Blane*)

The hotel has been replaced by the less impressive but pleasant-looking Roman Way tavern while the garage looks much the same. (*Robert Cook*)

The canal at Simpson lock, *c.* 1900. It was here, during the First World War, that the lock keeper's wife fell and died, the day after her 62-year-old husband had died from a long illness. The local press reported that Edith Mary Scott, 52, left her house to go to a shop on the other side of the canal, in darkness. She did not see that the bridge was open and stepped into the lock. Her husband, William Henry, was well known in angling circles and for many years was bailiff to the Coventry Fishing Club, whose members used Simpson waters. Mrs Scott was said to have been very tired from caring for her husband, but not suicidal. One of her sons had searched the house and raised the alarm.

The bridge had previously been very stiff but was recently serviced, which could have accounted for its partly open position. (*Colin Scott*)

Inset: Though this little enclave looks unchanged, we notice the chimney from an engine house has gone from behind the lock keeper's cottage and the canal side cottages are sought-after residences in this highly desirable location. The old hard ways of life have gone, hopefully along with the kind of wars that raged when Mrs Scott lost her life and fathers and sons were herded off to slaughter for the sake of empire and glory. (*Robert Cook*)

The canal, looking south toward Water Eaton, from Fenny Stratford bridge, offering an excellent view of Manor Fields in the 1920s. A corner of Valentine, Ord and Nagel's building is just in view on the right and a little swing bridge leads into a merchant's dock. The Grand Union was built between 1792 and 1800, bringing brief prosperity. Colin Scott did his apprenticeship at Nagels. He said: 'It was a dirty smelly place, lots of steam, electrics and gearboxes. Wonderful!' (*Colin Scott*)

Inset: A trendy new housing development obscures the old view across Manor Fields, and a pleasure barge departs from the marina and apartments which have replaced the old dock. Nagel's premises have also made way for something more modern, but the clean lines of the canal remain and there are still trees to be reflected in the still water. (*Robert Cook*)

Looking from near the tow-path, towards Fenny bridge, *c.* 1910. The swing bridge is to the right. Nagel's building rises grimly from the waterside and a barge pulls away from the wharf, probably having unloaded maize for the brewing process. The old Bridge Inn rises high beside the bridge after which it is named and large telegraph poles indicate that this is the all important Watling Street and the way to Holyhead. (*Martin Blane*)

Almost the same site, but viewed from the tow-path further back, the modern image shows the new development. Nagel's old building has gone but the Bridge Inn, with its dot.com advert painted on the white end wall, marks the spot. The canal bridge itself is part hidden in shadow on a bright May Sunday afternoon; light shimmering on the rippling canal adds a finishing touch. The swing bridge into the marina is visible on the right. (*Robert Cook*)

Saffron Street during VE Day celebrations, May 1945. In those days the Union Jack was a symbol of national pride and the spirit of a great nation. Some now fear it has been hijacked by extremists. (*Eddie Hancock*)

These days Saffron Street is still recognisable though fences and little personalised walls inform us of Thatcher's great council-house sell off, which did so much to create a shortage of affordable houses for the less well off while encouraging the myth of the property-owning democracy. (*Robert Cook*)

The cemetery at Fenny Stratford, *c.* 1910: a neat and tidy place where the quietness allows moments to reflect on the sad fact that all things are bounded and temporal. (*Pam Essam*)

A remarkably similar scene today apart from warnings that old vaults are unstable. The remaining chapel in this east-facing view is boarded up and also in disrepair. It was here that Doreen Dimmock discovered the worn-out memorial to local girl, 22-year-old Emma May Constable, who was fatally injured in a First World War munitions factory explosion in Luton. Locals helped her poor parents provide a headstone. Doreen made sure that a piece of local history was not going to be lost, motivating local funeral director John Matthews to arrange repair. (*Robert Cook*)

Eddie Hancock and friends pose for the camera after cricket on Water Eaton farmland during the late 1930s. (*Eddie Hancock*)

Eddie poses on the same spot, without his old friends, in June 2003. The long barn has been demolished and farmland was used for the Water Eaton Lakes Estate development, which took the first big waves of London overspill population. (*Robert Cook*)

Water Eaton village, south of Bletchley, *c.* 1900. (*Reg Knapp*)

Water Eaton village is much changed. So close to the canal, it has been a popular place for quality development and old properties have been modernised. Only an end of one of the old thatched properties is now visible from this spot and the open green has gone. Properties on the right and the road line are still enough to confirm that this is the same place. Dutch Elm disease rid the area of the trees years before. (*Robert Cook*)

5

City Way

Crime is a problem of urban life and Milton Keynes has its share. This is the Beacon trading estate, Fenny Stratford, on the Bletchley frontier. The warning sign is plain. Earlier warnings concerning the best provisions for the great influx of new city dwellers went unheeded. It was years before a hospital was built that even now struggles to cope, thus inspiring the joke that 'car thieves operate in this area, doctor's don't!'

Meanwhile, no expense is spared on retail and entertainment offerings that give Milton Keynes its glittering reputation among the middle, consumer and political classes. Opponents of further expansion warn that if services go the same way as manufacturing, the city will have an unemployment problem. In April 1964 the *Financial Times* urged more modest Bletchley expansion for a stable future, noting that the town had excellent communications, was near the M1 and was already cooperating with the London County Council regarding overspill and had shops for three times the current population. But, as the paper observed: 'The idea of paying £1,000 an acre for Bletchley land to redevelop when virgin land can be taken for £200 compulsory purchase under New Town legislation, it's not going to happen.' Thus Bletchley became a Milton Keynes suburb and part of the 'city way'. (*Robert Cook*)

St Mary's Hall on Major's Hill in Buckingham Road, February 2001. At one time Labour Party headquarters, it was put up for sale after use as a Salvation Army charity shop. Robert Maxwell lost the 1959 election for Labour when Bletchley was part of the Buckingham constituency. His printing business was booming and he was pushing local Labour Party finances to greater strength. In 1962 the party opened the new headquarters with, as Joe Haines put it in his Maxwell biography, 'a genuinely amazed Hugh Gaitskell [party leader] delivered to the site by helicopter, the latest Maxwell innovation for politicians like him with little time to spare. The building cost £20,000 and stood in grounds of 1½ acres.' (*Robert Cook*)

Maxwell went on to fight the autumn's 1964 election against Elaine Kellett, who Haines described as 'academically brilliant but politically shrill'. The author recalls sitting on the bonnet of Maxwell's campaign Land Rover as a boy, gaining an autograph and the impression that Maxwell was certainly not shrill or preoccupied with the academic. He had the common touch, appealing to the masses with simple slogans like 'let Harold and Bob finish the job' – not too much spin in those days but it worked for Maxwell and his equally gifted new leader Harold Wilson. Labour came to power eager for a swift decision on the new north Bucks overspill development, but it didn't listen to Maxwell even though Harold made a personal visit to Wilton Hall. Bletchley became a suburb and finally the old Labour HQ came tumbling down in 2003 as we see here. New Labour has no need for such old-fashioned edifices. Robert Maxwell died mysteriously in November 1991 – it appeared his political affairs had become much more complex. (*Robert Cook*)

Newton Longville toward Bletchley, 1964. The town's areas were first associated with London when the London Brick Company took over A.E. Lamb's Newton Longville brickworks in 1933. There were thirteen chimneys standing at the time of this picture and there is very little housing in view. (*Reg Knapp*)

Looking in the same direction today there are a few more houses but no chimneys. It is summer here and greenery obscures the outlook but there is remarkable similarity, even in the housing along the ridge. The brickworks was a big local employer, using the carboniferous Oxford clay which needed little additional fuel to burn and was pressed rather than moulded – called the Fletton process after where it was invented. The company originally provided large output for the expansion of London, hence the name. It was also a magnet to Londoners like the author's father, looking for a job and country life after a devastating world war.

The photographer described this image as being taken at the end of the brilliant summer of 1964; it was October. A London Brick Company lorry, immaculately turned out in red livery with black cab top, departs on to Newton Road with another load for the 1960s house-building boom. The 1960s were an age of dreams when anything seemed possible, and the 1950s were at last a memory. (*Reg Knapp*)

The trees fell victim to Dutch Elm disease in 1975/76, and the brickworks to Hanson Trust's cuts after they took over London Brick in 1984. Plans to redevelop the site have been slow coming and at one stage there was mention of reopening it as a brickworks if planning did not go through. Many were relieved to see the end of sulphurous fumes in an area that had become very built-up after postwar expansion, the views of newcomers conflicting with established industrial practice. Now the gates are well rusted and this is an area designated for further city growth. (*Robert Cook*)

Former Bletchley brickworker, the late Ray Akins, was once asked why brick workings were called knot holes. He joked back: 'Because after all the brick clay has been dug out it is not there any more!' At one time worked-out claypits made handy fishing places and were generously donated for the workers' leisure. Then came the consumer society and the growth of Milton Keynes. London Brick Company formed their Easidispose subsidiary and bid for the contract to receive new city waste. A different source of smell was thus engendered. This photograph shows the gates to the waste site during the early 1970s. (*Reg Knapp*)

The waste site is now operated by Shanks with a fleet of specialist vehicles and receiving bulk waste vehicles from many sources on a daily basis. A plan to build an incinerator on the site caused alarm and protests owing to its association with cancer, but population expansion and consumerism creates a waste disposal conundrum. Dustcart drivers also complain that it is very difficult to collect rubbish in streets congested by parked cars. (*Robert Cook*)

Beechcroft Road, off Newton Road, during Elizabeth II's 1953 Coronation celebrations. The drift towards London's city ways was already under way as Reg Knapp recalled in 1998: 'All the farms have gone. It was lovely to have a farm at the top of the garden in Beechcroft Road. We used to go out blackberry picking. I went up the garden one day and saw Farmer Ramsay over the hedge. I said "Would you mind if I cut it down a bit?" He said "You can do what you like. I've sold the field for building." That was quite a blow. The new houses changed things. We had anemones in the garden. I went up one day and they had gone. A mum had told her kids to take them!' (*Reg Knapp*)

The scene is a little different today with trees, high hedges and fences obscuring much of the original view. Hefty old paving slabs have been replaced by the ubiquitous and cheaper tarmac and the street sign has been moved to a more conspicuous position, a necessity as Bletchley grew in size, becoming absorbed in a new metropolis of busy people who might easily get lost along the way! (*Robert Cook*)

A derelict farm along Buckingham Road in May 1997, awaiting redevelopment. There is a powerful anti-farming lobby in Britain, often quoting that 80 per cent of the land is in the hands of farmers yet provides only 1 per cent of GDP. Countryside is devoured for development nationally at 11,000 hectares a year. Mrs Stanley remembers walking down Whaddon Way with her children to get apples from the farmer here, who she recalls was very friendly and didn't mind the children as long as they respected the countryside – but does the government respect it? (*Robert Cook*)

Wincanton Hill estate, May 2003, and the houses have been built and occupied for some years. Life moves fast around Bletchley. (*Robert Cook*)

Looking from Middlesex Drive towards the tower block of Mellish Court, early 1960s. A row of lock-up garages lines the vicinity of the present Hampshire Court. P.J. Stanley recalls how much easier it was to get about Bletchley before it all got built up and he had to rely on public transport. Those were the days when every TV break featured an advert about which soap powders washed whiter and the captive housewife was encouraged to be very competitive. The washing here looks very bright: was it Omo, Daz or Persil that did the trick? Or maybe it was Surf! (*P.J. Stanley*)

Trees block the outlook today but the flats are just visible and the houses which have replaced the old garages. Government is keen to get as many houses as possible into the south-east, setting out minimum densities of thirty per hectare for major new developments. Around here that won't make them cheap! (*Robert Cook*)

The Stanley family are having fun in the back garden of 139 Middlesex Drive during the 1960s, when the urge to pack the houses in was not so strong. Concessions were already being made to the age of mass car ownership, hence the line of garages. (*P.J. Stanley*)

Another generation of the family enjoying the same garden, now a much more established environment, giving a hint of the country that preceded the city way that now prevails. (*Robert Cook*)

Looking west across Whaddon Way, early 1960s. Georgina 'Gina' Ward is busy in her role of 'teacher'. Mrs Stanley recalls, after she had recently moved here and was walking back from the old Shoulder of Mutton pub: 'I heard these two ladies talking loudly so that I could hear. They said they were sick of Londoners coming to Bletchley and getting all the houses. I said if you mean me, I'm proud to say I was born and bred in Bucks, at Slough.' Sadly politicians changed that by putting Slough into Berkshire and not even Bletchley is Bucks any more. Phyllis Ward remembers when cows used to wander down Warwick Road, and her family used to cross the A5 to gravel pits and the kids pretended they were at the seaside, or walked into town via Bletchley Park and the kids paddled in the lake. (*P.J. Stanley*)

Inset: The same spot today and Georgina poses with P.J. Stanley. This intrepid lady said she has lived all over Bletchley but is happy to be back in Whaddon Way even though it has changed, with all the defensive hedges. She says the sense of community is not quite the same; she remembers when the neighbours all hired a spin drier to share for the weekend. Gina has even lived in Australia: 'I was queuing one day, for ages and this bloke pushed right in. When I complained he said "Fair dinkum lady, no queues here".' So it seems there is still something to be said for England in spite of its hurried city ways. (*Robert Cook*)

Children play in front of 110 Whaddon Way in the early 1960s. On 2 May 1964 Council Surveyor J.F. Smithie complained that not enough was being done by the county to support Bletchley's expansion. In December 1966 Housing Minister Robert Mellish visited the town to open a block of flats named after him. At a luncheon provided at Wilton Hall, he said he was sorry he could not say anything about the town's future. The public inquiry had yet to decide whether Bletchley would be the new city centre, as many objections were still being considered. In the same month council rents went up by 4s and Councillor T.J. Dickens said it was unfair, but predictions indicated it was needed to keep the budget £30,000 out of the red by the end of the financial year. (*P.J. Stanley*)

Trees, bushes and a realigned pavement have made the scene almost unrecognisable today. It looks like an oasis of calm in a busy place. P.J. Stanley was born nearby and recalls, with Georgina Ward, that it was a very friendly community. P.J. said that 'Everything changed when the Wiltshires got burgled. Everyone got dogs.' Traffic flow is heavy along this cut-through and in 1968 a total of £20,000 was allocated for parking bays.

Tricia Bates, *née* Stanley, poses with her young son Gary outside 139 Middlesex Drive in the mid-1960s. Bletchley has some interesting road and estate names. This one reflects the London origins of so many 1960s newcomers. (*P.J. Stanley*)

Another generation, but so much is the same. Sadly it is still difficult to find affordable homes around Milton Keynes, but that is nothing new. Back in January 1965 Mr D. Lee asked the Council: 'How long is the Council waiting list for people who don't come under the Greater London Council scheme?' 'Very long'. A local paper mentioned a woman who applied when she had a toddler, who was now eight; and she now had a 3-year-old as well as another on the way, but still no house. 'It's getting rather cramped in our flat,' she said. (*Robert Cook*)

Looking north in the early 1960s. Christopher Stanley in the garden of 139 Middlesex Drive with everything to look forward to. There is an unbelievable expanse of open countryside, but with modern equipment it won't take long to fill it. (*P.J. Stanley*)

P.J. Stanley and now it's all behind him. Bletchley kept on growing northward as did Milton Keynes. When plans for the new unofficial overspill city were announced, the *Bletchley Gazette* dismissed objectors with the words: 'To pooh-pooh the idea of a North Bucks city as a planner's pipe dream is to shut one's eyes to the population problem in south-east England of which the county forms part. . . . Here in Bletchley the city may find warmer support if the whole town itself becomes the springboard of the scheme. . . . There would be a certain justice in Bletchley, already a pioneer in overspill expansion, playing a major part when the country decides to follow its lead.' (*Robert Cook*)

Stephenson House dominates this 1995 view of Bletchley town centre development, dwarfing the Co-op. Milton Keynes has drawn high profile business away from here, as feared when Bletchley wasn't made the city centre, and office space is let with difficulty.

However, the town is still pressing ahead with innovations as this new construction site, rising up in the same location today, demonstrates. It will be home to a Wilkinson bargain store and a leisure facility. (*Robert Cook*)

Harrington's was a well-known trader for many years. The Victoria Road shop is seen here back in the early 1960s just before Brian Sidebottom took it over. It was very typical of the multifarious shops tucked away in Fenny Stratford's neat little streets. (*Brian Sidebottom*)

Brian Sidebottom renamed his business in line with the new city image. He is pictured here outside his shop in Victoria Road – the frontage having been considerably modified – just before retirement in July 2001. It is now a high performance motorcycle shop. (*Robert Cook*)

Harrington's shop interior just after Brian Sidebottom's takeover in the 1960s. It all looks rather quaint. (*Brian Sidebottom*)

Brian Sidebottom during the final days of his closing-down sale in July 2001; the olde worlde atmosphere remained here until the end. It's a far cry from the modern multiples but there are still plenty of quirky little shops in Fenny Stratford, like Miss Teas if you want a cuppa or Pollards in Aylesbury Street if you want good old-fashioned service and quality hardware and ironmongery. Of course Fenny has moved with the times too and there are plenty of exotic eateries in keeping with the multi-cultural nature of the city. Naughty names like Foxy Lady also sound inviting. In addition, a broad-minded attitude to sex has given us the Pink Punters club. (*Robert Cook*)

Benford's butcher's shop in Simpson Road, early 1930s. The slaughterhouse was at the rear. Doreen Dimmock recalled that you could buy lovely meat there. She added: 'Dad and uncle Percy rented a field down in Simpson for shooting rabbits and anything that came off the river was ours. Double-barrel shotguns and rifles were kept in a locked cabinet by the fireplace. I skinned the rabbits. It was a way of life. Dad sold them to old man Benford.' (*Glyn Lewis*)

Today Benford's attractive butcher's signs have gone. New City Heating is emblazoned on the gable end of the old shop. New city folk must be kept warm without the hard labour involved in the days when Eddie Hancock used to cut up firewood in these parts. All mod cons are a must. (*Robert Cook*)

William Webster and Harry Keyte's blacksmith's shop at the top of Duncombe Street. They ran
the smithy until William and his wife Sarah emigrated to Canada in 1908, where they settled
in the Victoria area of Vancouver Island. Duncombe Street was also home to Mrs Perring's
sweet and tobacco shop, which was popular with the railwaymen. Her eldest daughter had a
cake shop in the old tin shops near the railway bridge and goods yard. (*Daphne R. Atkins*)

The shop has been rebuilt and is yet another facility for car owners, bought by Nationwide
Autocentre. The flyover has been added and track realigned; part of the old line used to run
through the bordering terrace's gardens. (*Robert Cook*)

Labour Home Secretary David Hennels visiting Sherwood Drive fire station, 1969. Station Officer Greaves stands to his left. All looks very orderly, but fireman Colin Matthew recalled some tension when full timers, many of them GLC-sponsored newcomers to country ways, began taking over more and more of the 'shouts' (call-outs) from the retained men. There was also major upset during the 1977 strike. Colin remarked: 'People brought us wood for our fires as we sat picketing outside the station. They supported us. We went from a 56 hour week to 42 hours and got a 30 per cent pay rise.' (*Buckinghamshire Fire & Rescue*)

The scene outside the fire station in November 2002 is rather different, with fire-fighters back on strike for the first time since 1977, once again under a Labour government. It took until the summer of 2003 to settle the dispute, during which time the Deputy Prime Minister John Prescott mooted redundancies and issues of recruitment. Government blocked local authorities from settling, until finally both sides accepted an original local authority proposal for 16 per cent and talks on restructuring. Prescott suggested that fire-fighters' Queen's Golden Jubilee medals should be handed out without formal presentation or – better still – posted to recipients. (*Robert Cook*)

The retail trade is highly competitive in the new city area and rents high. This is particularly so in the home-improvement line, with so many firms moving in to serve homeowners and tenants in this rapidly growing city space. So the scene here in November 1997 is set to change. WH Smith's Do It All will soon be hauling down the flags on their Beacon estate branch with a view to selling the whole chain. (*Robert Cook*)

T.K. Maxx occupies the site today. All the big windows have gone and there is no need for flags outside what is mainly a budget price clothing store. It all looks mysterious from the outside, but inside a pleasant atmosphere prevails with fine displays of merchandise and comfortable music. (*Robert Cook*)

The A5 Watling Street, Fenny Stratford, looking towards Stony Stratford in the 1920s. The approaching car is in the vicinity of what is now Tesco's roundabout and the countryside is remarkably open in what was mainly farming country. London–Holyhead telegraph poles stand like sentries by the road which winds a little and climbs away towards Denbigh. (*Colin Scott*)

Inset: The scene is much changed today, with pavement and improved carriageway. A retail outlet has replaced the old Terrapin factory just left of the photographer. Tetley Tea and Rodex have made way for Tesco's and the supermarket roundabout is visible in the middle distance. Jack Cohen founded Tesco in 1959, rising with the Green Shield stamp gimmick. Now supermarkets are essential to the city way and

competition keen, with Tesco leading the field. Britain is more a nation of consumers than producers now, but there are still fine examples of manufacturing locally, like Jim Marshall's amplifier factory just beyond the trees and junction with Saxon Street on the left. Marshall was among the first to seize the business opportunities in Bletchley. Scott Meat is another great name now departed. A former employee said: 'I went on holiday in 1981, as usual in the last week of August and first week of September. I returned to the night shift and was greeted with "Hello Jim, you got yourself a new job yet?" "No" I said. "Well you'd better hurry, because we close in a fortnight." There was a lot of protest and Tony Benn came down, but we closed.' (*Robert Cook*)

A new boiler is delivered to Beacon Brushes factory, on the Watling Street, mid-1930s. Company Engineer Fred Scott is standing by the trailer which is parked outside Peake's clothing (which became Rodex) and opposite Beacon. (*Colin Scott*)

The site of the old Peake's factory, which was taken over by Rodex and was associated with Aquascutum and Jaeger brand names. It was demolished in the 1980s to make way for Tesco's, as seen here from the Beacon Retail Park. Doreen Dimmock remembers going to work at Rodex for 12s 1d a week in the late 1930s. 'I'd done a 5-year apprenticeship at Cowley and Wilson. They don't learn practical things now. We'd start at the bottom. A girl who started at the same time was on 25s. I finished at 5 p.m. Nowadays people want to start halfway up the ladder.' (*Robert Cook*)

Education used to be a matter for teachers like 'Barrel' Cook. But a mass age requires mass processing and the system to do it. It has become a political football and hot potato combined and there never seems to be enough money. Renaming things and chasing targets seem the best on offer and there is a high demand for further education, often because earlier stages fail to meet practical needs. Here we see the old College of Further Education, formerly the grammar school, being demolished in November 2002. (*Robert Cook*)

Now you see it, now you don't. The space, formerly part of Lord Leon's Bletchley Park, is cleared and a spanking new college renamed Bletchley Campus has been built to the left of the picture. Meanwhile the debate about raising standards continues and it's all very confusing. I asked a senior teacher what he thought. He said: 'Standards aren't falling, they are different.' (*Robert Cook*)

George Wilks and his horse Dolly *en route* along Simpson Road to Rowland's timber yard in 1962. St Martin's looks neat and tidy basking in the sunshine and 30-year-old traffic lights still control the A5 junction. Milton Keynes would require a whole new dual carriageway A5 bypass because Fenny would never cope. England had not quite started to swing and the road was narrow because the Rose and Crown, right, had yet to tumble to make room for city ways (see pp. 84–5). (*Colin Scott*)

This is recognisable as the same place today. The Swan Hotel, left, has been brightened up by white paint and the junction widened. Two mini roundabouts suffice to ease the junction and St Martin's still stands like a sentinel on the old Roman route. (*Robert Cook*)

Denbigh Bridge, at the end of the original London–Birmingham railway line, where travellers broke their journey, stopped at the inn and some local women seized the opportunity to ease male travellers' loneliness! This picture was taken on 1 August 1954 as an express train thundered over the bridge. Grass and signal-box look tidy. A man, maybe father or grandfather (people looked older in those days), accompanies a girl tricyclist, and a British car trundles north-westward towards a hoarding advertising Britain's biggest motor concern. Those were the days when Britain almost was an island! (*K. Barrow*)

Verges and hedges are not so cared for now; labour and machines are dear in a city of near full employment and with a taste for glamour. Still this spot is little changed. The signal-box has been ousted by new technology but the hoarding is still there. The week before this picture was taken, in June 2003, the advert was for the BBC *Spooks* programme, all about MI5 watching over us. Here it's another BBC offering of a revamped Basil Brush show, with a multi-cultural image. Advertising emphasis has shifted from manufacturing to entertainment, like the nation as a whole. Milton Keynes, the new city way, is very much about entertainment and shopping. (*Robert Cook*)

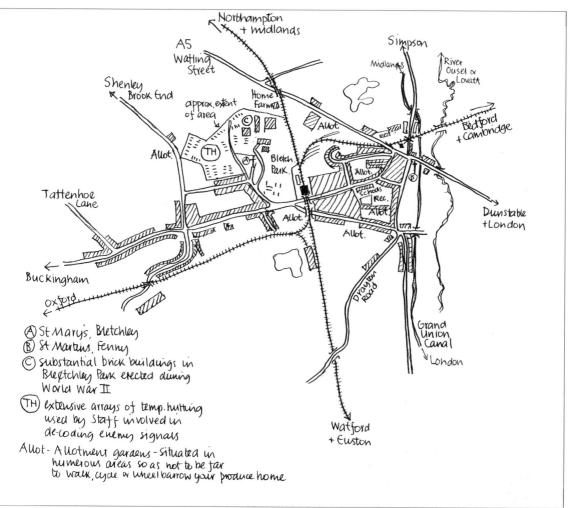

A sketch map of Bletchley in the late 1940s, just before the great expansion undertaken by Bletchley UDC and GLC to accommodate London overspill. The resultant housing and Denbigh Hall industrial estates gave the town the layout and looks it still maintains in 2003. (*Andrew Shouler*)

ACKNOWLEDGEMENTS & BIBLIOGRAPHY

I would like to thank all who have found the time to talk to me about Bletchley over the years. Without so many people donating or loaning photographs it would have been an impossible task and I thank them for their kindness. Their names are recorded under the photographs. So many have contributed to my understanding over the years that I hope I have not forgotten anyone.

Martin Blane has been my trusty guide around the byways for many years. Colin Scott and the Bletchley Historical and Archaeological Society have been erudite influences. Colin's photographic contribution was much appreciated. Pam Essam and Eileen Parker provided most valuable contributions to the photographic record and spent hours helping me to interpret them. Also I extend grateful thanks to Doreen Dimmock who recalled some sensitive and interesting moments from the long-lost past. Eddie Hancock was another wise guiding influence, happy to talk to me for hours and to walk around old haunts. I also took the liberty of recalling some valuable contributions from those who helped me with earlier books; Peter Stanley was a latecomer to the project but was most energetic and enthusiastic in his support, leading me to the acquaintance of Georgina Ward and her family, adding yet another dimension. Thanks are also due to Andrew Shouler for his fine maps and to Brian Sidebottom for his reminiscences. Once again I am indebted to Colin Stacey, Initial Photographics and the photographic legacy of the late Ken Barrow. Edwin Wilmshurst made a valuable contribution to the railway record. Additional thanks to Donald Fraser Blane and Roland Doggett for their help in the past which has contributed so obviously to this account. Also thanks are due to Bletchley Park and Derek Garvey. Final thanks are due to Simmons Aerofilms. I am sorry I could not find more room to display their fascinating studies of Bletchley from the air.

Cook, Robert, *Bletchley Voices*, Tempus, 1997
——, *Bletchley in Old Photographs*, Sutton, 1995
——, *Bucks Bricks*, Barracuda, 1997
—— & Shouler, Andrew. *Milton Keynes in the News*, Sutton/WH Smith, 2000
Grigg, A.E., *Railwayman's Tales of Old Bletchley*, Baron, 1996
——, *Job for Life*, Baron, 1993
——, *Bletchley Town of Trains*, Barracuda, 1980
Haines, Joe, *Maxwell*, Barracuda, 1980
Hill, Marion (ed), *Bigger Brighter Bletchley*, Living Archives, *c.* 1996